The Dream Kit

Also by Gayle Delaney, Ph.D.

Living Your Dreams
Breakthrough Dreaming: How to Tap the Power of
    Your 24-Hour Mind
New Directions in Dream Interpretation
Sensual Dreaming: How to Understand and Interpret
    the Erotic Content of Your Dreams

The

Dream Kit

An All-in-One ToolKit
for Understanding Your Dreams

Gayle Delaney, Ph.D.

HarperSanFrancisco
A Division of HarperCollins*Publishers*

FIRST EDITION

Library of Congress Cataloging-in-Publication Data
Delaney, Gayle M. V.
The dream kit : an all-in-one toolkit for understanding your
dreams / Gayle Delaney. — 1st ed.
p.   cm.
Accompanied by audiotape and 36 cards.
ISBN 0–06–251284–6 (pbk.)
1. Dream interpretation.   I. Title.
BF1091.D379   1995   95–7501
154.6'3—dc20   CIP

95 96 97 98 99 ❖GLO 10 9 8 7 6 5 4 3 2 1

Introduction

Your Dreams Have a Personal Meaning

We all dream at least four or five dreams every single night. When you dream you take a good look at your life—your relationships, your work, yourself. You use your own private picture language to express how you really feel and what you honestly think about the important issues in your life. Your dreams offer you timely and often surprisingly accurate assessments of your current circumstances. In your dreams you can experience the most amazing things. You can fly, talk to long-lost friends, travel through time, visit places of breathtaking beauty, and come to understandings about yourself or your relationships that are light-years ahead of your waking awareness. You can even solve problems by sleeping on them. Your *Dream Kit* is designed to help you tap this rich, natural resource. By using the tools in this kit, you will learn to interpret your dreams and begin to use them effectively in waking life.

Since your dreams are made up of images drawn from your own life experiences, no dream dictionary or fixed symbol system will give you the meaning of your dreams. In order to understand why you dreamt of your high school friend, Lynn, you must find out what she means to *you*. It's not important what she means to anyone else. Even when you dream of a well-known person such as Prince Charles or of a well-known place such as Texas, you will not know why until you find out exactly how *you* feel and think about them. Obviously, if your friend dreams of Prince Charles, and

1

she admires him and finds him attractive, it will mean something quite different than if you dreamt of him and you think he is cold, rigid, and unkind to his wife. If your friend was born in Texas and longs to return to her beloved state, her dream of Texas would express very different feelings from yours if you happen to think Texas is a state that is much too conservative for your tastes. No dream dictionary or traditional dream interpreter could ever do justice to your unique mix of feelings and thoughts, which give meaning to almost every image in your dreams. But you *can* learn how to ask yourself the right questions that will unlock the personal meanings in the dreams that fascinate and puzzle you.

Your *Dream Kit* will teach you how to interview yourself in a way that will lead you to the unique meaning of your dreams. In your kit you will find cue cards that you can lay out before you or hold in your hands as you work with a dream of your own or with a friend's dream. These cards will prompt you step by step through a dream interview, and they will provide you with good questions to ask yourself or your dream partner about each important element in the dream. You have many tools in your *Dream Kit*. I have designed them with great care after nearly two decades of specializing in dreamwork so that professionals and amateurs alike will have an easier time learning this very practical, nonideological way of working with dreams. Let's take a look at what is in your kit.

Begin by listening to the audio cassette, which will provide an overview of my unique program for understanding your dreams. Don't worry about memorizing the steps and techniques. They are all elaborated on later in this introduction.

Cassette Side A

On side A of the cassette I give a brief introduction to the fascinating world of dreams, followed by tips on how you can recall your dreams more vividly. Then I describe the dream interview approach to dream interpretation and tell you how you can become a dream interviewer yourself.

As side A continues, I explain how you can use the various tools in your *Dream Kit* to help understand your dreams. I walk you through the six steps of the dream interview and coach you in the most effective use you can make of your cue cards as you work with a dream, beginning with the Dream Interview Step Cards and the Dream Element Cards.

Cassette Side B

Side B continues the discussion of the tools in your *Dream Kit*. I begin with the Common Theme Cards, and then I explain how to use the Dream Analysis Sheets and Dream Review Sheets.

I then give instructions for the "dream incubation" process, in which you pick a problem before falling asleep and awaken with a dream that has helped you understand or solve that problem.

If you have trouble falling asleep, listen to the last part of side B of the tape, which will help you relax. You can listen to it for ten minutes as you fall asleep. You will find you get more and more relaxed each time you play the tape. Eventually you will probably be able to relax quite well and quickly on your own.

Most of us need about eight hours of sleep. Did you know that you have your longest twenty-five- to thirty-five-minute dreams in the eighth hour of sleep? Dr. William Dement, the chief of Stanford University's Sleep Research Center, believes that most Americans are chronically sleep deprived and therefore less efficient, more accident prone, and less able to incorporate new learning. You may need seven, eight, nine, or even ten hours of sleep a night. You will know that you are getting enough sleep if you awake without an alarm feeling refreshed and alert.

Here are a few simple things you can do to improve the quality and length of your sleep:

1. Remind yourself that sleep is not a waste of time. You solve problems in your sleep and generate dreams that offer you insights often far superior to those you have while awake. You refresh yourself, usually improve your mood, and increase your learning abilities while sleeping. So carve out time to get to bed earlier or to take naps in the afternoon. Once you adapt to a new sleep

schedule, you will wonder why you ever put up with too little sleep.

2. Create a wonderful sleeping environment. Is your mattress comfy? Not everyone needs a bed hard as a rock. These days you can find pillow-topped mattresses with a couple of very soft inches lying above a firm base for good back support. A less expensive alternative that still gives you a wonderful cradled feeling is a foam mattress pad placed under your regular mattress pad.

   Blacking out a room by installing blackout shades or curtains or wearing a good night mask will let you sleep, undisturbed by the puckish habit of the sun's early rising.

3. Exercise, but not just before sleep. Consider cutting out caffeine. Even one cup in the morning can disrupt your sleep habits. When you can rely on a cup of coffee to stimulate you out of that miserable grogginess you woke up with, you won't be motivated to get to bed early enough to awake feeling refreshed.

4. Create pleasing presleep habits. Slow down, listen to soothing music, take a bath, write in your dream journal, read relaxing materials, count your blessings. What you choose to do with your mind before sleep is perhaps the most important factor in determining how easily you fall asleep.

Sweet dreams!

Using Dreamwork Tools

Learning to tap the amazing resource of your dreams is exciting and fun, although it requires some practice. To begin, you need a simple tool, a dream journal.

Starting a Dream Journal

Get yourself a blank book or place three-holed paper on a clipboard to use as a dream journal. Divide each page as follows: Date, Day Notes, Title, Dream #1. At the top of the first page, enter today's date.

Day Notes

In the day notes section, jot down three or four lines about what you did and felt today. Try to briefly note the emotional highlights of the day. As you work with your dreams, you will find that writing down your day notes will improve your ability to recall vivid dreams. These notes will become very dear to you over time as a journal of your waking life and as a major source of clues to the meaning of your dreams, which almost always deal with issues from the preceding day.

In keeping your day notes, you need not go into detail. If you keep the notes brief, you will be more likely to record them almost daily and enjoy the process. For example, you might write that you had a lovely Sunday reading the newspaper and going for a bike ride. Then you felt relief and satisfaction at finishing a project for work but were angry at your friend who hurt your feelings by forgetting your birthday. Be specific about who and what triggered certain feelings without spending too much time and energy on the details, and you will almost always have enough information to remember the context that gave rise to a particular dream. When you find yourself working with a dream that you had a few years or even a few days before you interview yourself, you will find day notes written before, not after, you had the dream to be extremely helpful.

Dream Title

Leave this line empty until you have recorded a dream and have chosen a simple title that will help you recognize the dream at a glance.

Dream #1

Record your dream here. Write down whatever is in your mind as you awake. Even if you remember only a little fragment of a dream, write it down. Don't worry if you remember the dream in reverse with the last scene coming to mind first. You can reorder it later. Describe your dream as completely as possible. Take a moment and search for words that best describe the different feelings you had during each major moment of your dream.

If you recall no dream at all, be patient, let your mind wander, see if a dream surfaces. If not, write down one line about whatever thoughts and feelings come to mind. This will get you in the habit of paying attention to what you are thinking just as you awake, and this is the key to remembering your dreams. Some people want to remember a couple of dreams every day, while others might feel overwhelmed with more than two or three a week. If you remember and work with only one dream a week, you can still gain enough insight to be way ahead of the game.

If you don't want to wait until tomorrow morning to write out a dream, you can record one or more that you remember already. You may want to write down a dream from childhood, a recurring dream, or a dream from last week. Once you start writing, you may be surprised at how much you can remember. Don't forget to give each dream a title for easy reference.

Dream Incubation

Dream incubation is the process of setting yourself a problem before sleep and awakening the next morning with a solution—or with a dream that provides insights or ideas to move closer to the solution. (I offer examples of dream incubation on side B of the cassette tape.)

Almost everyone has gone to sleep with a problem in mind and at least once awakened with a solution to that problem. You can harness this natural problem-solving function of sleep and dreams by following these steps:

1. Choose a problem or creative challenge that is important to you.

2. Fill out a Dream Incubation Sheet (see below) by writing a little about your problem and coming up with a simple question that you write down and repeat to yourself as you fall asleep.

3. When you awake, write down whatever is in your mind, and see if you have the literal solution or a symbolic dream that might be about your issue.

4. If you recall a dream, record it and use your cue cards to interpret it. Once you know what the dream is about, see if it answers your incubation question. While you will usually be able to incubate a dream successfully, try to resist the temptation to assume that your dream is a direct response to your question. This may lead you to do a sloppy interview and to read into your dream

meanings that aren't there. If your incubation did not work, and if your dream is about something else, then it would be a shame to lose the insight the dream offers by force-fitting it to answer your question. You can always try the incubation the next night. If you ask for a dream on topic A and get a dream on topic B, then it may very well be that your dreaming mind thinks topic B is more important for you to understand at this time in your life.

Dream Incubation Sheet

Included in your *Dream Kit* are some Dream Incubation Sheets, which appear at the back of this book. Record today's date at the top of the first page.

Incubation Discussion

Write out four or five lines about your problem or about the idea you need. What is your problem, what are the issues involved, where do you feel stuck, and what are some possible solutions? If you worry about this problem, write down your concerns; this will help you relax better as you go to sleep.

Question or Request

Write out a one-line question that clearly states what you want your dream to help you understand or solve. Questions like "What shall I do with the rest of my life?" and "What is the meaning of life?" are too general and do not yield good results. Try questions that are more focused and specific, such as: "What keeps me from finding a career I like?" "How might I be sabotaging myself without realizing it?" "What keeps me from feeling free and exuberant?" "What characteristics do I need in a job, or a mate, to make me happy?" "I need a new idea for my project at school."

When you ask for a dream, you will get powerful insights if you are ready to look at how you play an important, if not always a causal, role in your difficulties.

Asking what you can do about your part in seemingly chance situations can empower you to make more enlightened choices and create a better life. Here are a few more questions the students at our dream center have found to be enlightening: "Why do I always pick men who are dead ends?" "Why do I pick friends who betray me?" "What are the main strengths and weaknesses of my relationship with my new boyfriend?" "What can I do to improve my marriage?"

Repeat your incubation question or phrase to yourself over and over as you fall asleep. Every time your mind wanders, come back to the phrase you wrote down and you will usually fall asleep quickly.

Dream #1

Record your dream here. Even if your dream puzzles you or if you don't see any relation to your question, write it all down. Until you interview yourself about the dream, don't make any judgments about the dream's meaning. After an open-minded interview, ask yourself if the dream answered your question. You may be surprised to discover that a dream of bizarre imagery provided a perfect metaphor or analogy for answering your question. Until you find out what your dream is about, you can't be sure whether or not your incubation was successful.

Comments

If you immediately see connections between your dream and your question, jot them down. You can find more ideas on how to incubate dreams and how to formulate questions about your self-image, your relationships, career, and creativity in my book *Living Your Dreams* (HarperSanFrancisco, 1988).

Nightly Dream Analysis Sheet

At the back of this book, you will find another of the tools in your *Dream Kit*, the Nightly Dream Analysis Sheet. When you have finished recording a dream in your journal, fill out one of these sheets. Be brief. Don't try to interpret the dream, just try to get an overview. These questions will help you see the structure of your dreams and will warm you up for your dream interview, which you can conduct when you have the time. You need not fill out a nightly analysis sheet for every dream. Work at your own pace, enjoy your explorations, and do only as much as you want to do and can fit into your schedule.

Let's look at the questions on this sheet.

Date and Title

This is simple.

Main Theme

Was this a dream of flying, drowning, running from an aggressor? Of needing help but being unable to call out? Identifying the theme of your dream will help you focus on the main point, and later when you review a dream series, it will show you recurring patterns.

Main Conflict or Challenge

In your dream, were you afraid you would be hurt, sad that you lost your friend? Were you trying to catch your bus but too disorganized to get to it on time? Were you in an argument with your mother or old girlfriend? Try to describe briefly the specific conflict of your dream.

Main Feelings

Be as specific as you can about the main feelings in your dream. Search for the words that best describe them—*angry, furious, frightened, petrified, happy, elated, turned on, repulsed, puzzled, shocked,* and so forth. If you find yourself using words like *frustrated* when you really mean *sad,* or *frightened* or *angry* when you really mean *hurt,* keep at it till you find the most accurate word. The surprising power of the right words will become clear to you as you progress.

Outcome

How did things come out in the end? Did you escape the mad dog, or was he about to have his way with you? Did you make friends with the person you first saw as an enemy? Were you killed? Did you figure out how to make the phone work? What were you left wondering?

Resources Used or Needed

When you got into a tight spot in the dream, how did you get out of it? Did you ask for help, run away, fight back? If things ended badly, can you say what would have saved the day? For example, did you or a main character in the dream do something stupid? Did you pack too much luggage so that your baggage prevented you from getting on the train? What resource might have saved the day? Help from a trusted friend? Better thinking or more courage on your part? Better preparations ahead of time or perhaps the willingness to discard some of your old baggage?

What Situations, Feelings, or People in Your Waking Life Come to Mind as You Describe the Elements in Your Dream?

The key to unlocking the meaning of your dreams is to make connections between the images in the dream to the events, people, and feelings in your waking life. In working with your *Dream Kit*, we will call these connections *bridges*. As you conduct a dream interview, you will learn to ask the questions that clarify the bridge from the dream to waking life. If you choose not to do a whole interview, you can use this space on the Nightly Dream Analysis Sheet to explore one or two images briefly. Sometimes, especially as you become more skilled as an interviewer, working with just a few images will unlock a whole dream for you.

Dream Review Sheets

Included in the back of this book are some tools for tracking patterns and themes in your dreams over an extended period of time. These tools include the Weekly and Monthly Dream Analysis Sheets, the Quarterly Dream Review, and the Annual Dream Review. By answering briefly the questions outlined on these sheets, you can gain important perspective on your dreams over time.

You will be surprised and delighted to see how much you learn by regularly reviewing your dreams and your day notes. You will notice recurring patterns that were invisible before, and you will begin to recognize metaphors and interpretations that just seem to pop out at you. At times, you might notice recurring images or themes that you have been consistently unable to understand. This will motivate you to make a special effort to unravel their meanings. As you spot important patterns in your dreams and in your life, you will be in a better position to change the patterns you don't like. Dream reviews are your best bet if you want to reinforce the insights you have gained and put them to work to improve the quality of your relationships and your life.

Your *Dream Kit* includes a month's worth of Nightly Dream Analysis Sheets and a year's worth of Weekly, Monthly, Quarterly, and Annual Sheets. Please feel free to copy these as necessary.

Now we move to the dream interview, the best way I have found to unlock the personal meaning of dreams.

The Dream Interview

To unlock the meaning of dreams, it is better to become a dream interviewer rather than a dream interpreter. Why? Because there are no fixed meanings for any dream images, and an interviewer's job is to discover rather than to impose meaning. Most interpretations derived from dictionaries or from rigid application of traditional psychological ideologies are inaccurate, ridiculously vague, or just plain wrong!

If you want to understand the meaning of a dream, I suggest you set up a "dream interview." The dreamer can ask a friend or therapist to play the part of the interviewer, or the dreamer can play both roles. The interviewer pretends to have just come from another planet and asks the dreamer a series of specific questions about the dream. Pretending that the interviewer is an alien is crucial. This device teaches the interviewer to keep his or her preconceived notions and prefabricated interpretations out of the interview. The job of the interviewer is to elicit from the dreamer what the dreamer thinks, feels, and senses about the dream and its connection to the dreamer's life. Further, the dreamer is much freer to discover and express his or her true feelings if the interviewer does not play the role of an authoritative, wise therapist who really has all the answers. The dreamer is the one who has the answers, and the interviewer's job is to help the dreamer discover that fact.

For example, suppose you had a dream about Jimmy Carter. You take your dream to a friend for interpretation. If your interpreter nods his or her head wisely and tells you that Jimmy Carter represents a father image, what good does that do you? If instead your interviewer from another planet asks you, "Who is Jimmy Carter, and what kind of guy is he?" you will learn much more. You might say that Jimmy was a president who didn't know how to work the Washington political machine, that he was naive and ineffectual. Then when your interviewer asks you if that description fits anyone in your life, you might feel surprised and say it fits you and how you have felt in your new job. Jimmy and your dream may have had nothing do with your father at all!

Or you might respond that Jimmy was a president of high integrity and good intent but was too weak to handle the national political system. Yet now you realize he is the only former president who continued to serve the country energetically through housing programs and expert diplomatic ventures. In this case, you might discover that your description of Jimmy reminds you of your father, whom you underestimated in your youth and whom you now appreciate as a very strong, principled, and active man. You can see that, even if you did use Jimmy to represent your father in your dream, an interpreter will miss very important characteristics that only you can come up with and that give specific meaning to your dream. You dreamt of Jimmy and not of Ronald Reagan or Richard Nixon, because your impressions of Jimmy made him the right man to carry the meaning for your dream message.

The students at our dream center in San Francisco, both professionals and amateurs, are constantly amazed at the descriptions they give to their interviewers and at the way those descriptions help them see what their dreams mean. Even when you interview yourself, which is the most common way to conduct a dream interview, pretending that your imaginary interviewer comes from another planet makes it much easier and quicker to uncover the personal meaning in your dreams. With practice, you will come to interview yourself almost automatically when you wake in the morning. Some of my students even interview themselves while they are dreaming, or they hear me asking them questions in their dreams!

The cue cards provided in your *Dream Kit* will aid you in becoming a skilled interviewer. Three sets of cards are provided. The Dream Interview Step Cards guide you through the six steps of a dream interview. The Dream Element Cards list questions you can ask to elicit a rich description of all the elements of the dream and find bridges between the dream and waking life. You can hold these cards in your hands as you work with a dream. They will prompt you to ask the right questions to execute each step of the interview. The Common Theme Cards list themes that most people dream about at some time during their lives. These cards provide questions to help you reflect on your own personal meaning of these common themes.

The first time you are ready to interpret one of your dreams or to help a friend with one of his or hers, take out your cue cards and read each one through once. Spread your Dream Interview Step Cards out in front of you.

Diagram Your Dream

Prepare for your interview by diagramming your dream. Sometimes dreams can seem confusing, disorganized, bizarre, and overwhelming. Where to begin? Actually, most dreams have structure and discrete elements that can be identified and worked with. Most dream elements can be grouped into one of six categories: settings, people, animals, objects, feelings, and actions/plots. Especially in the beginning of your practice as a dream interviewer, it will be easiest if you first highlight the different elements in the dream you are about to work with. Here's the way we do it at the dream center:

Draw a box around each major setting.

Circle each person.

Circle each animal.

Underline each major object.

Make a wavy line under each feeling.

Put a line with an arrow at the end under each major action or plot.

If you are working with a dream partner, be sure you both have a copy of the dream, which you can diagram together. This should take only a couple of minutes. Don't split hairs. If you are unsure how to mark an image, try the most likely marking, and if the questions for that element don't fit, try another category. For example, if you dream of Grandmother's house, you could either underline *Grandmother's house* as an object or draw a box around it as a setting. Asking the questions related to either object or setting will probably bring out the same feelings. You might prefer to first ask the questions on your People card about your grandmother, since the feelings you have about her house will probably have a lot to do with how you feel about her. If you come across a blended or transforming image in which, say, your friend Berta also looks like your sister or actually becomes your sister in the dream, ask the People questions about each one and then describe the composite image that includes both people's attributes. Quotes such as "Then he said, 'Get out of here' " are treated as actions.

How do you know which element to ask about first? It usually works best to take them in the order in which they appeared in the dream, so the clues you gather will follow the dramatic structure and development of your dream plot. As you gain experience you will be able to target certain key images and save time. Knowing how to do this takes practice, so in the beginning it is easiest to approach your dream elements in order of appearance.

Now we move to the six steps of a dream interview. Hold your Dream Element Cards in your hand or spread them out in front of you near the Dream Interview Step Cards. Place the Common Theme Cards in a pile nearby. If you have diagrammed a dream, you are ready to execute step one of a dream interview.

1. Description

Get a rich description of each of the major elements in the dream.

This is the most important step in the interview. If you are to find out what a particular image means to you, you must first find out what you think and feel about that image. What are its most salient features or characteristics, and how do you feel about them? Only after you have given a good description of an element can you really see what it stands for in your life. Dream images are metaphors. By dreaming of a finicky cat who won't come sit on your lap, you may be comparing your cold, distant, finicky boyfriend to that sort of cat. You may be saying to yourself, "Even though my boyfriend is cool and sleek and very attractive to me, he is like a cat, and I don't really like cats because they don't love me the way dogs do." Your dream metaphor, which compares your boyfriend to a cat, may help you see that this cool cat will never make you happy. So until you describe the cat and remind yourself of how you feel about cats, you won't be in a good position to see how the dream cat represents your boyfriend.

Your Dream Element Cards list the basic questions to ask yourself or the dreamer about each dream element. Keep the cards in your hands or spread out in front of you as you work with a dream.

The questions you will find on these cards have been carefully refined over two decades of teaching people how to understand their dreams. If you try asking the questions exactly as they are written, you will find that one word such as *like* can make all the difference. If you ask a dreamer, "What is John Wayne like?" the response will be more to the point and more personal than if you just say, "Who is John Wayne?" or "Tell me about John Wayne." If you ask someone to describe a snake, you won't get an answer that is nearly as clear, specific, and full of feeling as you will if you ask, "What is the snake in your dream like?" or "What is the personality of such a snake?"

One question you will never find on these cards is, "What does a _____ mean to you?" Even though this is what you want to find out, asking the question this way almost always interrupts the process. If you ask it of a friend you are interviewing, you will likely see a puzzled look in response; your friend wouldn't need an interviewer if she already knew the answer! She might hazard a response, but it will usually take the form of a half-baked, prefabricated, formulaic interpretation that fails to express her personal thoughts and feelings about the image. Remember that you, as interviewer, come from another planet and need to know first things first. Asking the dreamer for descriptions, not interpretations, for example, "Who is Tom Cruise?" or "What are motorcycles like?" will give you much more relevant and more accurate results.

Remember that a rich description of a dream element includes both thoughts and feelings. You are trying to elicit both the dreamer's beliefs about the facts of that element and his or her feelings about that image. If the answers you get are too long, ask the dreamer (or yourself) to summarize the description using three or four adjectives that most clearly express what he or she thinks and feels about the element. This will help you out in the next steps of the interview. If you find that you cannot elicit a rich description from yourself or your dreamer, make up additional questions aimed at getting the dreamer to verbalize his or her thoughts and feelings about the element.

Phrase your questions from the alien point of view, and you will be less likely to turn your interview into an inquisition. Be gentle, be curious. Spare your dreamer that dreadful wiser-than-thou attitude put on by so many therapists and would-be gurus. Most dreamers deeply appreciate an interviewer who respects their intelligence and who stays out of their way when it comes to making descriptions and interpretations. Dream interviewers make a point of not contaminating dreamer's private webs of feelings and associations with "helpful" and intrusive suggestions or interpretations. Instead, interviewers take pride in devising nonleading questions that help dreamers find their own words, which are tailor-made to trigger the dreamers' own recognition of the meaning of a dream. If you create an atmosphere of nonjudgmental curiosity to learn how the dreamer sees the world and how that worldview gives meaning to the dream, you and the dreamer will find much surprise, amusement, insight, and pathos in this work. (For more information on eliciting a good description, and on the entire dream interview method, see my book *Breakthrough Dreaming: How to Tap the Power of Your 24-Hour Mind*.)

The Common Theme Cards list questions you can ask to explore the personal meaning of common dreams. If the dream you are about to work on is the subject of one of these cards, try asking the Common Theme Card questions first. You may find that you can understand your dream without conducting a full interview.

2. Restatement

Restate or recapitulate to yourself or to your dreamer a concise version of the description you have obtained. Do not add your own words or associations—and certainly not your interpretations. Use the dreamer's exact words, and try to use the same tone and emphasis. Ask yourself or your dream partner if there is anything in your restatement that needs to be corrected, modified, or expanded. In this step (which takes places as you continue to use the Dream Element Cards), you are trying simply to play back to the dreamer his or her own words. If you restate the description well, you will be amazed to see how often the dreamer looks at you as if this is the first time she realizes what she has said. Now you are ready for the next step, which is also performed using your Dream Element Cards.

3. Bridge

Bridge from the dream image and its description to specific characters or situations in the dreamer's life. The bridging questions you find on your Dream Element Cards will be something like, "Does _____, which you describe as _____ (restate the description once again), remind you of anything, of anyone, or of any part of yourself?" Since we often use images of other people and even animals to highlight certain aspects of ourselves, it is a good idea to check out this possibility. Sometimes the person in the dream really represents that person. Sometimes a cigar is just a cigar. So if you dream of your girlfriend leaving you for another man, you may well be dreaming about your fears that she will leave you. If the description and restatement lead the dreamer to say that the dream image reminds him only of that person literally seen in the image, see if that interpretation seems accurate as you proceed with the dream. However, you can bet that if the person in the dream is not someone close to the current everyday life of the dreamer, that image likely represents either some part of the dreamer or some aspect of someone close to the dreamer. Sometimes the dreamer will not be able to bridge a dream image to anything or anyone or any part of himself. Maybe the dreamer is resisting the obvious, or maybe he is unable to grasp the metaphor. Or perhaps you and the dreamer did not elicit an adequate description. If you get stuck, you might want to go back to the description step and try again. Or you can go on to the next image and come back to this one later when you have gathered more clues from other dream elements.

In general, there is no need to hurry to the bridge step. You may want to execute the description and restatement steps for many elements before trying to bridge. This allows you to gather more information and momentum as you immerse yourself in the feelings and plot of the dream. Bridge when you think you are ready. If you bridge too early, and the dreamer can't make a bridge, just say, "Fine, we'll come back to it later, after we have gathered more clues." Your dreamer will not feel pressured, and you can carry on.

4. Test the Bridge

Test the strength of the bridge. Verify and clarify the parallels the dreamer sees between the dream element and her interpretation of it. A dreamer will sometimes make a bridge not because there is a good fit, but because he or she wants to please the interviewer. Have the dreamer tell you (or tell yourself if you are playing both roles) specifically how the dream element relates to the dreamer's waking life. Say something like, "You say this dream image reminds you of X. How so?" Dreamers will also sometimes bridge from only a small part of a description, ignoring the many other aspects of the dream image that don't seem to fit the waking situation well at all. Upon testing such a bridge, the dreamer can usually see that the dream image really doesn't correspond very well to the identified waking situation. When this occurs, simply return to the description and ask the dreamer to give it to you once again and to elaborate if appropriate. Then, armed with more information, restate and ask for a bridge again.

5. Summarize

Summarize descriptions and bridges as you go along, especially at the end of each scene and at the end of the interview. Ask the dreamer to correct you if you misstate or give an inappropriate emphasis to any part of the summary. Be sure to invite the dreamer to add any thoughts that occur to him or her as you are summarizing; these are often very helpful in integrating the pieces of the dream. As the dreamer listens to a summary or conducts one for herself or himself, the pieces of the dream should start to link together and continue to fall into place so that the overall thrust of the dream becomes clearer.

Encourage the dreamer to outline the parts of the dream that are still unclear to her. You may ask her a few questions to improve a description or repeat a restatement, or you could simply encourage her to wait a few days and see if some connections come to her. If you are working with a partner, try with all your might not to offer any interpretations of your own. While there are a few instances when this is helpful, usually it results in stealing from the dreamer the exquisite pleasure of figuring the dream out for herself.

6. Reflect

Reflect: Invite the dreamer (or yourself) to consider what, if any, actions or shifts in attitude might be appropriate in light of the insights gained from the dream interview. Be sure not to tell another dreamer what to do about the dream, and don't pressure yourself if you are working on your own dream. Ask the dreamer to reread the dream two or three times over the next week and deliberately keep in mind the major dream images and insights for the entire week. Writing a one-page summary of the dream interview is extremely useful. By putting in writing the thoughts and insights generated by your dreamwork, you are more likely to remember them and understand them better. Your dreams can give you priceless insights, but you must decide how and when to apply them if you want to make positive changes in your life. Changing your attitudes and behavior is rarely easy. It takes good insight and a leap, or many leaps, of true courage.

Now take another look at the Dream Interview Step Cards. Once you've got the steps clearly in mind, we'll take a look at a sample interview.

A Sample Dream Interview

Julia is a journalist. She came to me with the following dream. We diagrammed the dream this way, and Julia provided the dream title.

HOLE IN MY STOMACH

I am taking a bath in my apartment. Just as I start to relax, I notice a hole in my stomach with stuff coming out of it. I am concerned, but my mother says not to worry about it. She says it's time for me to get dressed and go to work. I get out of the tub and get ready to leave as she suggests. As I am leaving she smiles and says, "You know, you are going to be this way all your life." She means that I'll always have this hole in my stomach. I am distressed at her statement and at her smile. But I run downstairs and catch a cab to go pick up Marlo Thomas, whom I am to interview. I am excited to meet her at last.

Here is the interview I conducted with Julia about her dream. You can view it as a series of suggestions as to how you might use the interview questions on your cue cards.

> Gayle: Julia, why do you take baths? Pretend that I come from another planet and have no idea why humans do such a thing. (Description of an action question.)

> Julia: Okay. Well, I take baths rarely, but I love them. They are a good way to unwind. (Description of an action, taking baths.)

> G: (I decide to wait to ask restatement and bridge questions until we have gone further into the dream story. I go on to the next element.) You are in your current apartment? Is it your normal apartment in the dream? (I don't need a detailed description of the apartment if it is not modified in the dream.)

> J: Yes. Nothing unusual.

> G: So, you are in your home space taking a bath, which you usually do to unwind, right? (Restatement.)

> J: Right.

> G: Then what happens? (It's good to ask the dreamer to pick up the story line now and then. This reorients her to the atmosphere and action of the dream.)

> J: Well, as I start to relax, I notice this horrible hole in my stomach with all sorts of fluids and stuff coming out.

> G: So when you start to relax you notice this hole. Is that an important thing for a human to notice? What is wrong with having a hole in your stomach? (I didn't ask what a hole is, because that is too general to yield good results. Instead, I asked for a feeling- or judgment-oriented partial description about having a hole in the stomach.)

> J: It's life threatening. Very dangerous. If you leave it untreated, you lose your insides and die. (Description full of feeling and

judgment, but only partial. I have yet to find out why she dreamt of a hole in the stomach rather than in the heart, head, or intestines.)

G: What is a stomach? (Description question.)

J: It's where you digest your food so it can later send its nutrients to the rest of the body to keep you alive. (A good concrete description. I don't feel the need to ask her about her feelings about stomachs in general.)

G: So, you begin to relax and notice that you have a life-threatening hole in the part of you that digests your food and sends nutrients to your body to keep it alive, right? (Restatement of several elements together.)

J: Right.

G: How do you feel at this moment in the dream? (Description of a feeling.)

J: It's disgusting, and I am worried about it. Not as worried as I should be, however. I mean, I let my mom reassure me. (The dreamer describes how she feels about the hole and moves ahead to the image of her mom. I stay with the feeling for now and will ask about Mom later.)

G: Does this scene of being at home, taking a rare bath to relax, and then noticing this dangerous, life-threatening hole in your stomach remind you of anything or any situation in your life? (Bridge question for the whole scene.)

J: Oh yes. Now that I hear you saying all that, it reminds me of my overworking. (Bridge made.)

G: How so? (Testing the bridge.)

J: I almost never relax, but recently I have taken a three-day weekend and am noticing how anxious and stressed I am. My stomach is usually in knots. But as I think of this dream scene, it seems that my condition is worse than knots. I really am losing my stuff, my self. And I guess my lifestyle is life threatening. I am really not getting enough nutrients—other things besides work—in my life. (Strong bridge.)

G: What happens next?

J: My mother tells me not to worry and to get to work!

G: What is your mother like in this dream? (Description of a person. Since this is Mom, I focus the question to the dream role Mom plays. If I had just asked what Mom is like, we might have been here all day!)

J: Mom is just goal oriented. She wants me to be successful, and she is ignoring the seriousness of my problem. (Partial description.)

G: Is this what your mom is like in waking life? (Maybe the dreamer is dreaming about her relationship with her real mom, or perhaps she is using her mom to represent a part of herself. We'll see later.)

J: Oh, she's always been that way. And I've always followed her lead, just as in the dream I get dressed and go to work. (More description and a spontaneous bridge from the action of following Mom's suggestion in the dream to how she has done the same in waking life.)

G: Why would a mother say, "You know, you are going to be this way all your life"? And how do you feel about her saying this? (Action description question.)

J: She says it with a smile as if she doesn't care. Maybe she is getting some sort of revenge. She's certainly getting her way. I feel awful, distressed, unsupported. But I, like her, am glad to go off to such exciting work. So I cooperate. (Description of the actions of Mom's statement and of Julia's cooperation.)

G: So in the dream your mom is unsupportive of your problem and only focused on your work. She tells you with a smile that you will always have the hole in your stomach. (Restatement and summary.) Is there any part of you or anyone else in your life who acts like your mom in this way? (Bridge question.)

J: I guess I do. I treat myself much as my mom treated me when I was growing up. And since my mom doesn't live with me except in my dream, that must mean that she lives in my head.

G: You say you felt distressed and unsupported by her attitude. Do these feelings remind you of any similar feelings in waking life? (Bridge question for feelings.)

J: I can't say that I ever really was aware of feeling this way about Mom's attitude, though I should have as I was growing up. I just sort of accepted her attitude as normal. But now as I look at it, I feel distressed to see how I've been running my life and not taking care of my vital needs. (Here's a strong bridge, which doesn't need testing since the dreamer elaborated on it spontaneously.)

G: In the dream, both you and your mom are focused on your work. How do you feel as you grab a cab? (Feeling description question.)

J: I am excited about my work. It is glamorous. (Feeling description.)

G: Do these feelings remind you of anything? (Bridge question.)

J: Oh, sure. That is exactly what I love about my job. I interview famous and interesting people. (Bridge.)

G: Who is Marlo Thomas, and what is she like? (Description of a person question.)

J: Oh, she was my childhood model. She played a single, independent and happy, and glamorous young woman in a TV show.

I realize now that her happy and supportive work life and her happy romantic life was really a fantasy and that I shouldn't have believed in it so naively. But I did, and I modeled much of my life on her. (A rich description.)

G: So you modeled your life on your image of Marlo, whom you describe as single, independent, happy, and glamorous. You saw her as having a happy romantic and supportive work life. But now you think you shouldn't have believed so naively in such a fantasy. Right? (Restatement.)

J: Right.

G: So in the dream, you and your mom focus on work and don't take care of the hole in your stomach. Is there any way now that your fantasy about the Marlo Thomas happy life as a TV journalist is still leading you to ignore signs that you are working yourself to death? (Bridge question.)

J: It's so obvious now! I have known that I work too much, but the dream has made me realize how much I overdo it and why. I am as mean to myself as my mom was. I have let my childhood images of a fantasy role model blind me to the reality of my life. My work is not very supportive, I am stressed all the time, and I hardly have time for any romance at all. (Strong bridge, spontaneously elaborated.)

G: (In our actual interview I summarized the dream for Julia, then asked the following:) Well, in light of your realizations, are there any shifts in attitude or behavior that you would like to consider making? Or would you like to think about the dream for a few days before answering that question? (Invitation to reflect.)

J: You bet I'd like to make changes! This hole in my stomach is no joke. I am going to try to get my driving mom out of my life, or at least tame her. I am going to make time to relax and to live before it is too late.

G: Great. Good luck! Why don't we talk about your reflections in our session next week?

The next week Julia told me that her dream, the first she had ever worked on, was life changing. In one week's time she had come to recognize how often she hopped to her mother's orders, which regularly fired off in her head. She had begun to liberate some time in her schedule for non-work-related living, and she had begun to reassess the likelihood that her Marlo Thomas fantasy could ever win her a happy life. Not bad for a woman still in her twenties!

Nightmares and Recurring Dreams

Nightmares are red flags indicating that something is upsetting you, perhaps more than you admit, or that you are in an emotional situation that is dangerous to your well-being. Take advantage of your ability and willingness to remember a nightmare and interview yourself or ask a friend or therapist to interview you as soon as possible. You work with a nightmare just as you would any dream. Be prepared to deal with some upsetting thoughts so you can take a good look at the conflict that gave birth to the dream. This is a special opportunity to reassess your situation so you can do something to improve it. Very often our first realization that something is wrong comes in a dream. For example, if you have a terrible nightmare on your first day at a new job or after your first date with a new guy, you might be telling yourself to take a closer look at worries or problems you may be hiding from your conscious self. A bad dream can be a wonderful gift if you know how to understand and use it.

Recurring dreams are of two kinds. One is part of a post-traumatic stress syndrome. People who have been traumatized by war, rape, or other violence often have awful dreams of the traumatic events, and these tormenting replays can recur for years. But a few researchers have found that you can reduce their frequency by telling yourself during the day that the next time you have such a dream you will fight back and escape or conquer your attacker.

A more common form of recurring dream is an odd or scary dream about any theme that recurs in various forms over weeks or years. If you have one of these recurring dreams, write out the most recent version and interview yourself about it. Then look through your dream journal and see what your day notes reveal about the days that preceded each occurrence of the dream. If you are just starting to keep day notes, be sure to note the same thing in the future. If you keep good day notes, you will usually pick up important clues from them. For example, say you have recurring dreams of a vampire, whom you cannot find the will to resist. If you see in your day notes that the day before each vampire dream you were with one or another boyfriend whom you know is or was bad for you (perhaps he was pathologically controlling or jealous), then you will have a good hint to the meaning of your dreams. Our recurring dreams show us that we are stuck in repetitive, usually destructive, patterns. The dreams can open our eyes to these patterns so we have a better chance of changing them.

Oh Yes, and a Word About Sexual Dreams

Everyone has sexual dreams. Everyone wonders what they mean. And almost everyone is too embarrassed to talk about them. Sexual dreams often use sex as a metaphor to reveal to us our feelings about our important emotional relationships. Other sexual dreams help us explore our sexual inhibitions as well as our erotic potential. Perhaps the most basic quality of sexual dreams is they regularly present us with the opportunity to learn how to talk about things and feelings sexual. In a culture with so much sexual abuse of children, who often grow up with debilitating emotional scars, we need to teach families how to talk in healthy ways about sexual concerns. Sexual abuse can thrive only in homes where sex is a dirty secret. Learning to talk about your sexual dreams will help to break this cultural cycle and encourage a more sane and robust attitude toward an omnipresent factor in all our lives.

If you have sexual dreams that pair sex with violence and coercion, these probably upset you quite a bit. If so, see an experienced psychologist or psychiatrist for a few sessions to get some expert help in understanding them. Sometimes, but not always, these dreams indicate early sexual abuse that is continuing to impinge on the dreamer's sense of well-being and ability to form good love relationships. Sometimes such dreams are the one thing that motivates the dreamer to seek help and support.

Should you tell your steamy, romantic, sexy dreams to your spouse or sweetheart? Well, that depends. If you are hiding secrets, don't. If you want to share your deepest concerns, desires, hopes, and fears with the one you love, maybe. Both partners must realize that sexual dreams are not usually just wishes but a complex expression of the dreamer's most private and honest feelings about love, intimacy, and sex. If you and your partner know how dreams work and that by sharing them you will get to know each other at the deepest levels, then sharing all your dreams, including your sexual ones, will tremendously enrich the intimacy and trust you share. If you both are sensitive, careful, and honest, you will learn a great deal about what your partner wants and needs in a sexual and intimate relationship. (See my book *Sensual Dreaming* if you would like to know more.)

The Adventure of Dreams

Fill out your periodic dream review sheets as often as you can. You will be surprised and delighted to see how much you learn by regular reviews of your dreams and your day notes. You will notice recurring patterns that were invisible to you before and you will begin to recognize metaphors and interpretations that just seem to fall into place. At times you might notice recurring images or themes that you have been consistently unable to understand. This will motivate you to make a special effort to unravel their meanings. As you spot important patterns in your dreams and in your life, you will be in a better position to change the patterns you don't like. Dream reviews are your best bet if you want to reinforce the insights you have gained and put them to work to improve the quality of your relationships and your life.

Be patient with yourself as you learn about dreaming and about yourself. See if you can find a dream partner or a dream study group. The support and encouragement of other dreamers is wonderful and will speed your learning. Keep reading good books on dreaming, and take classes in dreamwork if they are offered in your area.

May your dream explorations bring you thrilling adventures, practical insights, and a deeper, sweeter appreciation of life and love. May you come up with wonderful new ideas and ingenious solutions to many problems, and may your sense of humor about yourself flourish.

Nightly Dream Analysis Sheet

Date:

Dream Title:

Main Theme:

Main Conflict or Challenge:

Main Feelings:

Outcome:

Resources Used or Needed:

What situations, feelings, or people in your waking life come to mind as you describe the elements in your dream?

Nightly Dream Analysis Sheet

Date:

Dream Title:

Main Theme:

Main Conflict or Challenge:

Main Feelings:

Outcome:

Resources Used or Needed:

What situations, feelings, or people in your waking life come to mind as you describe the elements in your dream?

Nightly Dream Analysis Sheet

Date:

Dream Title:

Main Theme:

Main Conflict or Challenge:

Main Feelings:

Outcome:

Resources Used or Needed:

What situations, feelings, or people in your waking life come to mind as you describe the elements in your dream?

Nightly Dream Analysis Sheet

Date:

Dream Title:

Main Theme:

Main Conflict or Challenge:

Main Feelings:

Outcome:

Resources Used or Needed:

What situations, feelings, or people in your waking life come to mind as you describe the elements in your dream?

Nightly Dream Analysis Sheet

Date:

Dream Title:

Main Theme:

Main Conflict or Challenge:

Main Feelings:

Outcome:

Resources Used or Needed:

What situations, feelings, or people in your waking life come to mind as you describe the elements in your dream?

Nightly Dream Analysis Sheet

Date:

Dream Title:

Main Theme:

Main Conflict or Challenge:

Main Feelings:

Outcome:

Resources Used or Needed:

What situations, feelings, or people in your waking life come to mind as you describe the elements in your dream?

Nightly Dream Analysis Sheet

Date:

Dream Title:

Main Theme:

Main Conflict or Challenge:

Main Feelings:

Outcome:

Resources Used or Needed:

What situations, feelings, or people in your waking life come to mind as you describe the elements in your dream?

Nightly Dream Analysis Sheet

Date:

Dream Title:

Main Theme:

Main Conflict or Challenge:

Main Feelings:

Outcome:

Resources Used or Needed:

What situations, feelings, or people in your waking life come to mind as you describe the elements in your dream?

Nightly Dream Analysis Sheet

Date:

Dream Title:

Main Theme:

Main Conflict or Challenge:

Main Feelings:

Outcome:

Resources Used or Needed:

What situations, feelings, or people in your waking life come to mind as you describe the elements in your dream?

Nightly Dream Analysis Sheet

Date:

Dream Title:

Main Theme:

Main Conflict or Challenge:

Main Feelings:

Outcome:

Resources Used or Needed:

What situations, feelings, or people in your waking life come to mind as you describe the elements in your dream?

Nightly Dream Analysis Sheet

Date:

Dream Title:

Main Theme:

Main Conflict or Challenge:

Main Feelings:

Outcome:

Resources Used or Needed:

What situations, feelings, or people in your waking life come to mind as you describe the elements in your dream?

Nightly Dream Analysis Sheet

Date:

Dream Title:

Main Theme:

Main Conflict or Challenge:

Main Feelings:

Outcome:

Resources Used or Needed:

What situations, feelings, or people in your waking life come to mind as you describe the elements in your dream?

Nightly Dream Analysis Sheet

Date:

Dream Title:

Main Theme:

Main Conflict or Challenge:

Main Feelings:

Outcome:

Resources Used or Needed:

What situations, feelings, or people in your waking life come to mind as you describe the elements in your dream?

Nightly Dream Analysis Sheet

Date:

Dream Title:

Main Theme:

Main Conflict or Challenge:

Main Feelings:

Outcome:

Resources Used or Needed:

What situations, feelings, or people in your waking life come to mind as you describe the elements in your dream?

Nightly Dream Analysis Sheet

Date:

Dream Title:

Main Theme:

Main Conflict or Challenge:

Main Feelings:

Outcome:

Resources Used or Needed:

What situations, feelings, or people in your waking life come to mind as you describe the elements in your dream?

Nightly Dream Analysis Sheet

Date:

Dream Title:

Main Theme:

Main Conflict or Challenge:

Main Feelings:

Outcome:

Resources Used or Needed:

What situations, feelings, or people in your waking life come to mind as you describe the elements in your dream?

Nightly Dream Analysis Sheet

Date:

Dream Title:

Main Theme:

Main Conflict or Challenge:

Main Feelings:

Outcome:

Resources Used or Needed:

What situations, feelings, or people in your waking life come to mind as you describe the elements in your dream?

Nightly Dream Analysis Sheet

Date:

Dream Title:

Main Theme:

Main Conflict or Challenge:

Main Feelings:

Outcome:

Resources Used or Needed:

What situations, feelings, or people in your waking life come to mind as you describe the elements in your dream?

Nightly Dream Analysis Sheet

Date:

Dream Title:

Main Theme:

Main Conflict or Challenge:

Main Feelings:

Outcome:

Resources Used or Needed:

What situations, feelings, or people in your waking life come to mind as you describe the elements in your dream?

Nightly Dream Analysis Sheet

Date:

Dream Title:

Main Theme:

Main Conflict or Challenge:

Main Feelings:

Outcome:

Resources Used or Needed:

What situations, feelings, or people in your waking life come to mind as you describe the elements in your dream?

Nightly Dream Analysis Sheet

Date:

Dream Title:

Main Theme:

Main Conflict or Challenge:

Main Feelings:

Outcome:

Resources Used or Needed:

What situations, feelings, or people in your waking life come to mind as you describe the elements in your dream?

Nightly Dream Analysis Sheet

Date:

Dream Title:

Main Theme:

Main Conflict or Challenge:

Main Feelings:

Outcome:

Resources Used or Needed:

What situations, feelings, or people in your waking life come to mind as you describe the elements in your dream?

Nightly Dream Analysis Sheet

Date:

Dream Title:

Main Theme:

Main Conflict or Challenge:

Main Feelings:

Outcome:

Resources Used or Needed:

What situations, feelings, or people in your waking life come to mind as you describe the elements in your dream?

Nightly Dream Analysis Sheet

Date:

Dream Title:

Main Theme:

Main Conflict or Challenge:

Main Feelings:

Outcome:

Resources Used or Needed:

What situations, feelings, or people in your waking life come to mind as you describe the elements in your dream?

Nightly Dream Analysis Sheet

Date:

Dream Title:

Main Theme:

Main Conflict or Challenge:

Main Feelings:

Outcome:

Resources Used or Needed:

What situations, feelings, or people in your waking life come to mind as you describe the elements in your dream?

Nightly Dream Analysis Sheet

Date:

Dream Title:

Main Theme:

Main Conflict or Challenge:

Main Feelings:

Outcome:

Resources Used or Needed:

What situations, feelings, or people in your waking life come to mind as you describe the elements in your dream?

Nightly Dream Analysis Sheet

Date:

Dream Title:

Main Theme:

Main Conflict or Challenge:

Main Feelings:

Outcome:

Resources Used or Needed:

What situations, feelings, or people in your waking life come to mind as you describe the elements in your dream?

Nightly Dream Analysis Sheet

Date:

Dream Title:

Main Theme:

Main Conflict or Challenge:

Main Feelings:

Outcome:

Resources Used or Needed:

What situations, feelings, or people in your waking life come to mind as you describe the elements in your dream?

Weekly Dream Review Sheet

Week of _____

List any recurring dream elements (settings, people, animals, objects, actions, or themes).

Have there been any recurring outcomes?

List any recurring feelings and note if they match any waking feelings you have had this week.

Which dream of the week seems most important to you? Why?

Any interpretations or comments?

Weekly Dream Review Sheet

Week of _____

List any recurring dream elements (settings, people, animals, objects, actions, or themes).

Have there been any recurring outcomes?

List any recurring feelings and note if they match any waking feelings you have had this week.

Which dream of the week seems most important to you? Why?

Any interpretations or comments?

Weekly Dream Review Sheet

Week of _____

List any recurring dream elements (settings, people, animals, objects, actions, or themes).

Have there been any recurring outcomes?

List any recurring feelings and note if they match any waking feelings you have had this week.

Which dream of the week seems most important to you? Why?

Any interpretations or comments?

Weekly Dream Review Sheet

Week of _____

List any recurring dream elements (settings, people, animals, objects, actions, or themes).

Have there been any recurring outcomes?

List any recurring feelings and note if they match any waking feelings you have had this week.

Which dream of the week seems most important to you? Why?

Any interpretations or comments?

Weekly Dream Review Sheet

Week of _____

List any recurring dream elements (settings, people, animals, objects, actions, or themes).

Have there been any recurring outcomes?

List any recurring feelings and note if they match any waking feelings you have had this week.

Which dream of the week seems most important to you? Why?

Any interpretations or comments?

Weekly Dream Review Sheet

Week of _____

List any recurring dream elements (settings, people, animals, objects, actions, or themes).

Have there been any recurring outcomes?

List any recurring feelings and note if they match any waking feelings you have had this week.

Which dream of the week seems most important to you? Why?

Any interpretations or comments?

Weekly Dream Review Sheet

Week of _____

List any recurring dream elements (settings, people, animals, objects, actions, or themes).

Have there been any recurring outcomes?

List any recurring feelings and note if they match any waking feelings you have had this week.

Which dream of the week seems most important to you? Why?

Any interpretations or comments?

Weekly Dream Review Sheet

Week of _____

List any recurring dream elements (settings, people, animals, objects, actions, or themes).

Have there been any recurring outcomes?

List any recurring feelings and note if they match any waking feelings you have had this week.

Which dream of the week seems most important to you? Why?

Any interpretations or comments?

Weekly Dream Review Sheet

Week of _____

List any recurring dream elements (settings, people, animals, objects, actions, or themes).

Have there been any recurring outcomes?

List any recurring feelings and note if they match any waking feelings you have had this week.

Which dream of the week seems most important to you? Why?

Any interpretations or comments?

Weekly Dream Review Sheet

Week of _____

List any recurring dream elements (settings, people, animals, objects, actions, or themes).

Have there been any recurring outcomes?

List any recurring feelings and note if they match any waking feelings you have had this week.

Which dream of the week seems most important to you? Why?

Any interpretations or comments?

Weekly Dream Review Sheet

Week of _____

List any recurring dream elements (settings, people, animals, objects, actions, or themes).

Have there been any recurring outcomes?

List any recurring feelings and note if they match any waking feelings you have had this week.

Which dream of the week seems most important to you? Why?

Any interpretations or comments?

Weekly Dream Review Sheet

Week of _____

List any recurring dream elements (settings, people, animals, objects, actions, or themes).

Have there been any recurring outcomes?

List any recurring feelings and note if they match any waking feelings you have had this week.

Which dream of the week seems most important to you? Why?

Any interpretations or comments?

Weekly Dream Review Sheet

Week of _____

List any recurring dream elements (settings, people, animals, objects, actions, or themes).

Have there been any recurring outcomes?

List any recurring feelings and note if they match any waking feelings you have had this week.

Which dream of the week seems most important to you? Why?

Any interpretations or comments?

Weekly Dream Review Sheet

Week of _____

List any recurring dream elements (settings, people, animals, objects, actions, or themes).

Have there been any recurring outcomes?

List any recurring feelings and note if they match any waking feelings you have had this week.

Which dream of the week seems most important to you? Why?

Any interpretations or comments?

Weekly Dream Review Sheet

Week of _____

List any recurring dream elements (settings, people, animals, objects, actions, or themes).

Have there been any recurring outcomes?

List any recurring feelings and note if they match any waking feelings you have had this week.

Which dream of the week seems most important to you? Why?

Any interpretations or comments?

Weekly Dream Review Sheet

Week of _____

List any recurring dream elements (settings, people, animals, objects, actions, or themes).

Have there been any recurring outcomes?

List any recurring feelings and note if they match any waking feelings you have had this week.

Which dream of the week seems most important to you? Why?

Any interpretations or comments?

Weekly Dream Review Sheet

Week of _____

List any recurring dream elements (settings, people, animals, objects, actions, or themes).

Have there been any recurring outcomes?

List any recurring feelings and note if they match any waking feelings you have had this week.

Which dream of the week seems most important to you? Why?

Any interpretations or comments?

Weekly Dream Review Sheet

Week of _____

List any recurring dream elements (settings, people, animals, objects, actions, or themes).

Have there been any recurring outcomes?

List any recurring feelings and note if they match any waking feelings you have had this week.

Which dream of the week seems most important to you? Why?

Any interpretations or comments?

Weekly Dream Review Sheet

Week of _____

List any recurring dream elements (settings, people, animals, objects, actions, or themes).

Have there been any recurring outcomes?

List any recurring feelings and note if they match any waking feelings you have had this week.

Which dream of the week seems most important to you? Why?

Any interpretations or comments?

Weekly Dream Review Sheet

Week of _____

List any recurring dream elements (settings, people, animals, objects, actions, or themes).

Have there been any recurring outcomes?

List any recurring feelings and note if they match any waking feelings you have had this week.

Which dream of the week seems most important to you? Why?

Any interpretations or comments?

Weekly Dream Review Sheet

Week of _____

List any recurring dream elements (settings, people, animals, objects, actions, or themes).

Have there been any recurring outcomes?

List any recurring feelings and note if they match any waking feelings you have had this week.

Which dream of the week seems most important to you? Why?

Any interpretations or comments?

Weekly Dream Review Sheet

Week of _____

List any recurring dream elements (settings, people, animals, objects, actions, or themes).

Have there been any recurring outcomes?

List any recurring feelings and note if they match any waking feelings you have had this week.

Which dream of the week seems most important to you? Why?

Any interpretations or comments?

Weekly Dream Review Sheet

Week of _____

List any recurring dream elements (settings, people, animals, objects, actions, or themes).

Have there been any recurring outcomes?

List any recurring feelings and note if they match any waking feelings you have had this week.

Which dream of the week seems most important to you? Why?

Any interpretations or comments?

Weekly Dream Review Sheet

Week of _____

List any recurring dream elements (settings, people, animals, objects, actions, or themes).

Have there been any recurring outcomes?

List any recurring feelings and note if they match any waking feelings you have had this week.

Which dream of the week seems most important to you? Why?

Any interpretations or comments?

Weekly Dream Review Sheet

Week of _____

List any recurring dream elements (settings, people, animals, objects, actions, or themes).

Have there been any recurring outcomes?

List any recurring feelings and note if they match any waking feelings you have had this week.

Which dream of the week seems most important to you? Why?

Any interpretations or comments?

Weekly Dream Review Sheet

Week of _____

List any recurring dream elements (settings, people, animals, objects, actions, or themes).

Have there been any recurring outcomes?

List any recurring feelings and note if they match any waking feelings you have had this week.

Which dream of the week seems most important to you? Why?

Any interpretations or comments?

Weekly Dream Review Sheet

Week of _____

List any recurring dream elements (settings, people, animals, objects, actions, or themes).

Have there been any recurring outcomes?

List any recurring feelings and note if they match any waking feelings you have had this week.

Which dream of the week seems most important to you? Why?

Any interpretations or comments?

Weekly Dream Review Sheet

Week of _____

List any recurring dream elements (settings, people, animals, objects, actions, or themes).

Have there been any recurring outcomes?

List any recurring feelings and note if they match any waking feelings you have had this week.

Which dream of the week seems most important to you? Why?

Any interpretations or comments?

Weekly Dream Review Sheet

Week of _____

List any recurring dream elements (settings, people, animals, objects, actions, or themes).

Have there been any recurring outcomes?

List any recurring feelings and note if they match any waking feelings you have had this week.

Which dream of the week seems most important to you? Why?

Any interpretations or comments?

Weekly Dream Review Sheet

Week of _____

List any recurring dream elements (settings, people, animals, objects, actions, or themes).

Have there been any recurring outcomes?

List any recurring feelings and note if they match any waking feelings you have had this week.

Which dream of the week seems most important to you? Why?

Any interpretations or comments?

Weekly Dream Review Sheet

Week of _____

List any recurring dream elements (settings, people, animals, objects, actions, or themes).

Have there been any recurring outcomes?

List any recurring feelings and note if they match any waking feelings you have had this week.

Which dream of the week seems most important to you? Why?

Any interpretations or comments?

Weekly Dream Review Sheet

Week of _____

List any recurring dream elements (settings, people, animals, objects, actions, or themes).

Have there been any recurring outcomes?

List any recurring feelings and note if they match any waking feelings you have had this week.

Which dream of the week seems most important to you? Why?

Any interpretations or comments?

Weekly Dream Review Sheet

Week of _____

List any recurring dream elements (settings, people, animals, objects, actions, or themes).

Have there been any recurring outcomes?

List any recurring feelings and note if they match any waking feelings you have had this week.

Which dream of the week seems most important to you? Why?

Any interpretations or comments?

Weekly Dream Review Sheet

Week of _____

List any recurring dream elements (settings, people, animals, objects, actions, or themes).

Have there been any recurring outcomes?

List any recurring feelings and note if they match any waking feelings you have had this week.

Which dream of the week seems most important to you? Why?

Any interpretations or comments?

Weekly Dream Review Sheet

Week of _____

List any recurring dream elements (settings, people, animals, objects, actions, or themes).

Have there been any recurring outcomes?

List any recurring feelings and note if they match any waking feelings you have had this week.

Which dream of the week seems most important to you? Why?

Any interpretations or comments?

Weekly Dream Review Sheet

Week of _____

List any recurring dream elements (settings, people, animals, objects, actions, or themes).

Have there been any recurring outcomes?

List any recurring feelings and note if they match any waking feelings you have had this week.

Which dream of the week seems most important to you? Why?

Any interpretations or comments?

Weekly Dream Review Sheet

Week of _____

List any recurring dream elements (settings, people, animals, objects, actions, or themes).

Have there been any recurring outcomes?

List any recurring feelings and note if they match any waking feelings you have had this week.

Which dream of the week seems most important to you? Why?

Any interpretations or comments?

Weekly Dream Review Sheet

Week of _____

List any recurring dream elements (settings, people, animals, objects, actions, or themes).

Have there been any recurring outcomes?

List any recurring feelings and note if they match any waking feelings you have had this week.

Which dream of the week seems most important to you? Why?

Any interpretations or comments?

Weekly Dream Review Sheet

Week of _____

List any recurring dream elements (settings, people, animals, objects, actions, or themes).

Have there been any recurring outcomes?

List any recurring feelings and note if they match any waking feelings you have had this week.

Which dream of the week seems most important to you? Why?

Any interpretations or comments?

Weekly Dream Review Sheet

Week of _____

List any recurring dream elements (settings, people, animals, objects, actions, or themes).

Have there been any recurring outcomes?

List any recurring feelings and note if they match any waking feelings you have had this week.

Which dream of the week seems most important to you? Why?

Any interpretations or comments?

Weekly Dream Review Sheet

Week of _____

List any recurring dream elements (settings, people, animals, objects, actions, or themes).

Have there been any recurring outcomes?

List any recurring feelings and note if they match any waking feelings you have had this week.

Which dream of the week seems most important to you? Why?

Any interpretations or comments?

Weekly Dream Review Sheet

Week of _____

List any recurring dream elements (settings, people, animals, objects, actions, or themes).

Have there been any recurring outcomes?

List any recurring feelings and note if they match any waking feelings you have had this week.

Which dream of the week seems most important to you? Why?

Any interpretations or comments?

Weekly Dream Review Sheet

Week of _____

List any recurring dream elements (settings, people, animals, objects, actions, or themes).

Have there been any recurring outcomes?

List any recurring feelings and note if they match any waking feelings you have had this week.

Which dream of the week seems most important to you? Why?

Any interpretations or comments?

Weekly Dream Review Sheet

Week of _____

List any recurring dream elements (settings, people, animals, objects, actions, or themes).

Have there been any recurring outcomes?

List any recurring feelings and note if they match any waking feelings you have had this week.

Which dream of the week seems most important to you? Why?

Any interpretations or comments?

Weekly Dream Review Sheet

Week of _____

List any recurring dream elements (settings, people, animals, objects, actions, or themes).

Have there been any recurring outcomes?

List any recurring feelings and note if they match any waking feelings you have had this week.

Which dream of the week seems most important to you? Why?

Any interpretations or comments?

Weekly Dream Review Sheet

Week of _____

List any recurring dream elements (settings, people, animals, objects, actions, or themes).

Have there been any recurring outcomes?

List any recurring feelings and note if they match any waking feelings you have had this week.

Which dream of the week seems most important to you? Why?

Any interpretations or comments?

Weekly Dream Review Sheet

Week of _____

List any recurring dream elements (settings, people, animals, objects, actions, or themes).

Have there been any recurring outcomes?

List any recurring feelings and note if they match any waking feelings you have had this week.

Which dream of the week seems most important to you? Why?

Any interpretations or comments?

Weekly Dream Review Sheet

Week of _____

List any recurring dream elements (settings, people, animals, objects, actions, or themes).

Have there been any recurring outcomes?

List any recurring feelings and note if they match any waking feelings you have had this week.

Which dream of the week seems most important to you? Why?

Any interpretations or comments?

Weekly Dream Review Sheet

Week of _____

List any recurring dream elements (settings, people, animals, objects, actions, or themes).

Have there been any recurring outcomes?

List any recurring feelings and note if they match any waking feelings you have had this week.

Which dream of the week seems most important to you? Why?

Any interpretations or comments?

Weekly Dream Review Sheet

Week of _____

List any recurring dream elements (settings, people, animals, objects, actions, or themes).

Have there been any recurring outcomes?

List any recurring feelings and note if they match any waking feelings you have had this week.

Which dream of the week seems most important to you? Why?

Any interpretations or comments?

Weekly Dream Review Sheet

Week of _____

List any recurring dream elements (settings, people, animals, objects, actions, or themes).

Have there been any recurring outcomes?

List any recurring feelings and note if they match any waking feelings you have had this week.

Which dream of the week seems most important to you? Why?

Any interpretations or comments?

Weekly Dream Review Sheet

Week of _____

List any recurring dream elements (settings, people, animals, objects, actions, or themes).

Have there been any recurring outcomes?

List any recurring feelings and note if they match any waking feelings you have had this week.

Which dream of the week seems most important to you? Why?

Any interpretations or comments?

Monthly Dream Review Sheet

Month:

List the elements that have recurred in your dreams this month.

Have you noticed any developments or changes in your dream characters or themes? Do these changes reflect changes in your life or in your attitudes?

What are the dream images you most want to keep in mind in the future? Why?

What are the most important things you have learned from your dreams this month?

In light of the above, have you made any changes or would you like to make any changes in your life? Which ones?

Monthly Dream Review Sheet

Month:

List the elements that have recurred in your dreams this month.

Have you noticed any developments or changes in your dream characters or themes? Do these changes reflect changes in your life or in your attitudes?

What are the dream images you most want to keep in mind in the future? Why?

What are the most important things you have learned from your dreams this month?

In light of the above, have you made any changes or would you like to make any changes in your life? Which ones?

Monthly Dream Review Sheet

Month:

List the elements that have recurred in your dreams this month.

Have you noticed any developments or changes in your dream characters or themes? Do these changes reflect changes in your life or in your attitudes?

What are the dream images you most want to keep in mind in the future? Why?

What are the most important things you have learned from your dreams this month?

In light of the above, have you made any changes or would you like to make any changes in your life? Which ones?

Monthly Dream Review Sheet

Month:

List the elements that have recurred in your dreams this month.

Have you noticed any developments or changes in your dream characters or themes? Do these changes reflect changes in your life or in your attitudes?

What are the dream images you most want to keep in mind in the future? Why?

What are the most important things you have learned from your dreams this month?

In light of the above, have you made any changes or would you like to make any changes in your life? Which ones?

Monthly Dream Review Sheet

Month:

List the elements that have recurred in your dreams this month.

Have you noticed any developments or changes in your dream characters or themes? Do these changes reflect changes in your life or in your attitudes?

What are the dream images you most want to keep in mind in the future? Why?

What are the most important things you have learned from your dreams this month?

In light of the above, have you made any changes or would you like to make any changes in your life? Which ones?

Monthly Dream Review Sheet

Month:

List the elements that have recurred in your dreams this month.

Have you noticed any developments or changes in your dream characters or themes? Do these changes reflect changes in your life or in your attitudes?

What are the dream images you most want to keep in mind in the future? Why?

What are the most important things you have learned from your dreams this month?

In light of the above, have you made any changes or would you like to make any changes in your life? Which ones?

Monthly Dream Review Sheet

Month:

List the elements that have recurred in your dreams this month.

Have you noticed any developments or changes in your dream characters or themes? Do these changes reflect changes in your life or in your attitudes?

What are the dream images you most want to keep in mind in the future? Why?

What are the most important things you have learned from your dreams this month?

In light of the above, have you made any changes or would you like to make any changes in your life? Which ones?

Monthly Dream Review Sheet

Month:

List the elements that have recurred in your dreams this month.

Have you noticed any developments or changes in your dream characters or themes? Do these changes reflect changes in your life or in your attitudes?

What are the dream images you most want to keep in mind in the future? Why?

What are the most important things you have learned from your dreams this month?

In light of the above, have you made any changes or would you like to make any changes in your life? Which ones?

Monthly Dream Review Sheet

Month:

List the elements that have recurred in your dreams this month.

Have you noticed any developments or changes in your dream characters or themes? Do these changes reflect changes in your life or in your attitudes?

What are the dream images you most want to keep in mind in the future? Why?

What are the most important things you have learned from your dreams this month?

In light of the above, have you made any changes or would you like to make any changes in your life? Which ones?

Monthly Dream Review Sheet

Month:

List the elements that have recurred in your dreams this month.

Have you noticed any developments or changes in your dream characters or themes? Do these changes reflect changes in your life or in your attitudes?

What are the dream images you most want to keep in mind in the future? Why?

What are the most important things you have learned from your dreams this month?

In light of the above, have you made any changes or would you like to make any changes in your life? Which ones?

Monthly Dream Review Sheet

Month:

List the elements that have recurred in your dreams this month.

Have you noticed any developments or changes in your dream characters or themes? Do these changes reflect changes in your life or in your attitudes?

What are the dream images you most want to keep in mind in the future? Why?

What are the most important things you have learned from your dreams this month?

In light of the above, have you made any changes or would you like to make any changes in your life? Which ones?

Monthly Dream Review Sheet

Month:

List the elements that have recurred in your dreams this month.

Have you noticed any developments or changes in your dream characters or themes? Do these changes reflect changes in your life or in your attitudes?

What are the dream images you most want to keep in mind in the future? Why?

What are the most important things you have learned from your dreams this month?

In light of the above, have you made any changes or would you like to make any changes in your life? Which ones?

Quarterly Dream Review Sheet

Dreams from _____ to _____

Which images and themes seem most important to you? Why?

How do they parallel waking concerns?

List, as specifically as you can, the insights you have gained.

What actions on these insights have you taken or have yet to take to improve your situation?

List any dream images or themes that don't yet make sense to you so you can put extra energy into spotting them and interviewing yourself about them later, especially if they recur.

Quarterly Dream Review Sheet

Dreams from _____ to _____

Which images and themes seem most important to you? Why?

How do they parallel waking concerns?

List, as specifically as you can, the insights you have gained.

What actions on these insights have you taken or have yet to take to improve your situation?

List any dream images or themes that don't yet make sense to you so you can put extra energy into spotting them and interviewing yourself about them later, especially if they recur.

Quarterly Dream Review Sheet

Dreams from _____ to _____

Which images and themes seem most important to you? Why?

How do they parallel waking concerns?

List, as specifically as you can, the insights you have gained.

What actions on these insights have you taken or have yet to take to improve your situation?

List any dream images or themes that don't yet make sense to you so you can put extra energy into spotting them and interviewing yourself about them later, especially if they recur.

Quarterly Dream Review Sheet

Dreams from _____ to _____

Which images and themes seem most important to you? Why?

How do they parallel waking concerns?

List, as specifically as you can, the insights you have gained.

What actions on these insights have you taken or have yet to take to improve your situation?

List any dream images or themes that don't yet make sense to you so you can put extra energy into spotting them and interviewing yourself about them later, especially if they recur.

Annual Dream Review Sheet

Dreams from _____ to _____

What trends do you notice in your dreams? How do these trends connect to your waking life?

Describe the most important things you have learned from your dreamwork this year.

List any positive changes you have made in your attitudes, behaviors, relationships, or career.

Describe the areas in your life where you still feel stuck or unhappy.

Make up incubation questions about these frustrating or unhappy issues so you can work on them in the future.

Dream Incubation Sheet

Date:

Incubation Discussion:

Question or Request:

Dream #1:

Comments

Dream Incubation Sheet

Date:

Incubation Discussion:

Question or Request:

Dream #1:

Comments

Dream Incubation Sheet

Date:

Incubation Discussion:

Question or Request:

Dream #1:

Comments

Dream Incubation Sheet

Date:

Incubation Discussion:

Question or Request:

Dream #1:

Comments

Dream Incubation Sheet

Date:

Incubation Discussion:

Question or Request:

Dream #1:

Comments

Dream Incubation Sheet

Date:

Incubation Discussion:

Question or Request:

Dream #1:

Comments

Dream Incubation Sheet

Date:

Incubation Discussion:

Question or Request:

Dream #1:

Comments

Dream Incubation Sheet

Date:

Incubation Discussion:

Question or Request:

Dream #1:

Comments

Dream Incubation Sheet

Date:

Incubation Discussion:

Question or Request:

Dream #1:

Comments

Dream Incubation Sheet

Date:

Incubation Discussion:

Question or Request:

Dream #1:

Comments

Dream Incubation Sheet

Date:

Incubation Discussion:

Question or Request:

Dream #1:

Comments

Dream Incubation Sheet

Date:

Incubation Discussion:

Question or Request:

Dream #1:

Comments

Dream Incubation Sheet

Date:

Incubation Discussion:

Question or Request:

Dream #1:

Comments

Dream Incubation Sheet

Date:

Incubation Discussion:

Question or Request:

Dream #1:

Comments

Dream Incubation Sheet

Date:

Incubation Discussion:

Question or Request:

Dream #1:

Comments

Dream Incubation Sheet

Date:

Incubation Discussion:

Question or Request:

Dream #1:

Comments

Dream Incubation Sheet

Date:

Incubation Discussion:

Question or Request:

Dream #1:

Comments

Dream Incubation Sheet

Date:

Incubation Discussion:

Question or Request:

Dream #1:

Comments

Dream Incubation Sheet

Date:

Incubation Discussion:

Question or Request:

Dream #1:

Comments

Dream Incubation Sheet

Date:

Incubation Discussion:

Question or Request:

Dream #1:

Comments

Dream Incubation Sheet

Date:

Incubation Discussion:

Question or Request:

Dream #1:

Comments

Dream Incubation Sheet

Date:

Incubation Discussion:

Question or Request:

Dream #1:

Comments

Dream Incubation Sheet

Date:

Incubation Discussion:

Question or Request:

Dream #1:

Comments

Dream Incubation Sheet

Date:

Incubation Discussion:

Question or Request:

Dream #1:

Comments

Dream Incubation Sheet

Date:

Incubation Discussion:

Question or Request:

Dream #1:

Comments

Dream Incubation Sheet

Date:

Incubation Discussion:

Question or Request:

Dream #1:

Comments

Dream Incubation Sheet

Date:

Incubation Discussion:

Question or Request:

Dream #1:

Comments